thank you

I have so many people to thank for helping with this book: Vanessa Pitsikas, for being a designer wise, composed and talented beyond her years; food editors Justine Poole, Steve Pearce and Jane Collings and their dedicated team of recipe testers for dishes that elicit oohs and aahs every time; copy editor Kirsty McKenzie for always asking the right questions; the amazing Con Poulos, talented Chris Court and all the other photographers whose images shine on every page; and, of course, to the *donna hay magazine* staff for being all-round superstars – your loyalty, creativity and professionalism help make donna hay a truly world-class brand. Many thanks must also be extended to Phil Barker and Peter Byrne at News Magazines; and to the team at HarperCollins. Thank you, thank you to friends old and new and my dear family. And to the men in my life: my wonderful sons Angus and Tom who make my heart soar, and my partner, Bill.

on the cover
front: crushed raspberry tart, page 54
back: rhubarb and vanilla crumble, page 46

Fourth Estate
An imprint of HarperCollins*Publishers*

First published in Australia and New Zealand in 2007,
by Fourth Estate, an imprint of HarperCollins*Publishers*
HarperCollins*Publishers* Australia Pty Limited
25 Ryde Road, Pymble, Sydney, NSW 2073, Australia
ABN 36 009 913 517

HarperCollins*Publishers*
31 View Road, Glenfield, Auckland 10, New Zealand

Copyright © Donna Hay 2007. Design copyright © Donna Hay 2007
Photographs copyright © Con Poulos 2007 cover, pages 1, 4, 7, 9, 10, 11, 12, 13, 14, 15, 16, 17, 19, 20, 23, 25, 27, 29, 31 (right), 33, 34, 35 (right), 37, 38, 39, 41, 43, 44 (left), 45, 47, 51, 52, 55, 56, 57, 59, 61, 62, 63, 67, 69, 70, 71 (right), 73, 74, 75, 77, 79 (left), 80, 83, 85, 87, 96, back cover; copyright © Chris Court pages 24 (right), 35 (left), 49, 53 (right), 71 (left), 81, 87; copyright © Lisa Cohen pages 44 (right), 53 (left), 79 (right); copyright © Ben Dearnley page 24 (left); copyright © Luke Burgess page 21; copyright © Brett Stevens pages 31 (left), 65.

Designer: Vanessa Pitsikas
Copy Editor: Kirsty McKenzie
Food Editors: Justine Poole, Steve Pearce, Jane Collings
Consulting Art Director: Sarah Kavanagh

Reproduction by Graphic Print Group, South Australia
Produced in Hong Kong by Phoenix Offset on 157gsm Chinese Matt Art.
Printed in China.

The rights of Donna Hay and the photographers of this work have been asserted by them under the *Copyright Amendment (Moral Rights) Act (2000).*

National Library of Australia Cataloguing-in-Publication data:
Hay, Donna.
Fruit.
Includes index.
ISBN 978 0 7322 8580 7.
ISBN 0 7322 8580 1.
1. Cookery (Fruit). I. Title. (Series : Simple essentials).
641.64

07 08 09 10   10 9 8 7 6 5 4 3 2 1

donna hay

SIMPLE ESSENTIALS

fruit

FOURTH ESTATE

contents

introduction   6

basics   8

breakfasts + preserves   18

desserts   32

pies + tarts   50

cakes + bakes   68

glossary   88

conversion chart   91

index   92

introduction

When I was a child I looked forward to the first mango of the season with the kind of anticipation usually reserved for Christmas or birthdays. What I couldn't articulate then, but now fully understand, is that the best things in life are truly worth waiting for. And so it is with fruit. Waiting for the peak of the season and selecting specimens which have recently been harvested means you'll be rewarded with the taste sensation of maximum juice, flavour and texture. We've reviewed our all-time favourite recipes to bring together this great collection of simple-to-prepare fruit-based treats. So spoil your family and friends and share the joy of a fruitful existence.

Donna

basics

With vibrant colours, heady fragrance and delectable
sweetness, it takes very little effort to make fruit the star
of any recipe. Here is our definitive guide to the fruits most
commonly used in this book, with loads of information on
selection and storage plus a range of tips for simple but
effective finishing touches.

all about fruit

In an ideal world, all our fruit would ripen on the tree or vine and travel straight from the farm gate to the plate. In the real world we can try to approximate this by knowing how to choose fruit at its peak and store it under optimum conditions.

peaches

Peaches reach juicy perfection in late spring and summer. There are white and yellow clingstone varieties as well as freestone (slipstone) peaches whose flesh can be twisted away from the stone. While today's market and production methods favour yellow varieties, many argue that a perfectly ripe white peach is superior in flavour, perfume and juiciness. Choose fruit that is firm and blemish free, but yields slightly when gently pressed. Peaches also deteriorate quite quickly, so eat as soon as possible after purchase.

nectarines

A type of peach without the fuzzy skin, nectarines come in slipstone and clingstone versions. The flesh colour ranges from white and yellow to an almost reddish orange. A summer through to autumn favourite, choose richly coloured plump fruit with smooth and glossy skin which has no tinges of green. One of the best guides to perfect ripeness is fragrance. Store nectarines in a single layer at room temperature to ripen, then keep for a maximum of a couple of days in the fridge.

apricots + plums

With their soft, downy skin ranging in colour from yellow to deep orange, apricots are another of summer's gifts. Choose evenly coloured fruit and store at room temperature. Plums are at their best from summer to late autumn. Skin colour ranges from almost purple to red and flesh from green and yellow to deep orange. Sugar plums are dried to make prunes. Japanese or blood plums, with ultra-sweet flesh yielding a deep red juice, are mostly considered cooking fruit, but they can also be enjoyed fresh.

red berries

Luscious strawberries are available year round though they actually peak during the summer months. Choose fruit that have their hulls intact, are red all over and have a bright glossy sheen. Raspberries are another of summer's delicate delights. They should be deep red and plump in appearance. All berries ferment quickly so check the bottom of the punnet to ensure there are no mouldy or squashed fruit. Store berries in the fridge in a single layer on a plate lined with kitchen paper and covered with plastic wrap.

berries

Blackberry hybrids, including loganberries, youngberries and boysenberries, have extended the season from late spring through to early autumn. If choosing fruit for jam, select some which are not so ripe to ensure a higher level of pectin, the important setting agent. Store in the refrigerator in a single layer on a plate lined with kitchen paper and covered with plastic wrap. Blueberries should have pale green flesh and plump, waxy purple skins. Summer is their peak but they are also available in the adjoining seasons.

cherries

Ranging in colour from yellow with red blushes to bright red and deep purplish black, cherries are one of summer's fleeting joys. Choose fruit that are plump with shiny skins, preferably with their stems intact (as they keep much better this way). Best consumed as soon as possible after picking, cherries can be stored in the refrigerator for a couple of days. Cherries oxidise quickly after slicing or stoning, though the browning process can be delayed by dipping the fruit in lemon juice.

apples

There are more than 7000 varieties of apples worldwide. Green apples, prized for their tart flavour and crunch, tend to hold texture and flavour when cooked. The sweeter red varieties, sometimes preferred as eating apples, also respond well to cooking. Apples come into season in autumn and last through winter. Choose fruit that are heavy for their size, with shiny skins and no blemishes. Small apples keep better than large ones and all apples lose crispness faster at room temperature than when kept in the fridge.

pears

The peak pear season runs from autumn through to spring. Pears continue to ripen from the inside after picking, so choose plump firm fruit with no spots and store at room temperature until the skin changes colour. Ripe pears can be kept in the refrigerator for several days, but are best eaten fairly quickly. Skin colour ranges from green and yellow to brown with russet tinges. Red skins are popular when presentation is paramount. For cooking, choose pears that are just ripe, because fully ripe fruit can become mushy.

bananas

Grown in tropical regions around the world, the banana is a staple of the South Pacific region where both the long Cavendish variety and the short, sweeter Lady Finger and sugar bananas grow in abundance. Dark green to black plantains are a cornerstone of the Caribbean and South American kitchens. The peak season is autumn, though bananas are available year round. Green tips mean the fruit is not completely ripe, while fruit with some brown specks is considered at its prime. Store at room temperature to ripen.

oranges

Prized for their high levels of vitamin C, oranges are available year round with some varieties fruiting in summer and others in winter. The blood orange is an autumn bearing Mediterranean variant, with dramatic ruby juice that is less acidic than that of regular oranges. Select fruit with firm skin that feel heavy for their size and show no evidence of mould, brown marks or wrinkling. Store in a cool, dry spot. You can expect to keep citrus for several weeks at room temperature and extend the life by storing in the fridge.

lemons + limes

Lemons are prized for their tart flavour and acidic juice. While the small, round, dark green Mexican or key lime is regarded as the "true" lime, the green yellow Tahitian lime is popular because it's seedless and yields plenty of juice. Like most citrus, lemons and limes peak from winter through to spring, but are available year round due to their long storage capacity. The juice of lemons and limes holds the acidic flavour, but the oil in the rind imparts the fragrance. Choose fruit with firm skin and no signs of bruising or mould.

quinces

Cooking transforms this hard, bitter, white-fleshed fruit into tender, fragrant, rosy pink morsels. Autumn is the peak season and shoppers should select firm fruit that feels heavy in the hand. If cooking quinces whole, be sure to remove any of the grey bloom that develops on the skin. When poaching, it's important to keep the quince submerged in the liquid, otherwise it will oxidise and turn brown. The best way to do this is to push a piece of baking paper into the pan and onto the surface of the liquid to stop the fruit floating to the top.

melons

It just wouldn't be summer without melons – luscious pink watermelon, heady fragrant orange rockmelons (cantaloupes) and green and juicy honeydews. Melons belong to the same family as squash and pumpkins, so select fruit that is slightly soft at the flower end and has a sweetish smell from the stalk end. They don't ripen further after picking, so choose fruit that has good colour and undamaged skin. Store melons at room temperature, but after cutting, cover with plastic wrap and keep in the refrigerator. Eat within a couple of days.

lychees, rambutans + starfruit

The rough reddish-skinned lychee has sweet, pearly-white flesh surrounding an elongated brown stone. Its cousin, the rambutan, takes its name from the Indonesian word, *rambut*, meaning "hair". Lychees and rambutans are high in vitamin C and best in summer. Choose fruit that is firm to the touch and store in the refrigerator. The waxy-skinned starfruit or carambola is another exotic treat, at its peak in autumn with high acidity and loads of flavour.

pineapples, mangoes + papayas

In kitchens the world over the mango heralds the arrival of summer. Ripe fruit is slightly soft to touch and strongly perfumed. Prized varieties have bright orange flesh free of fibrous strands. Rough skinned pineapple is another native of the tropics and available year round. A short crown of spiky leaves indicates a "roughie", valued for its juicy sweetness. Papaya is a red pawpaw available from autumn to spring. Unripe fruit is bitter, so choose papaya that "gives" under gentle pressure.

passionfruit + kiwifruit

Sweet fragrant passionfruit with myriad edible seeds are available year round, though they're best in autumn. Choose fruit that feel heavy for their size. Wrinkled skin can indicate ripeness in thin-skinned varieties. Store in a cool, dry spot for up to a week, or in the fridge if you want to keep them longer. The kiwifruit, or Chinese gooseberry, evolved in China, but has migrated to New Zealand and the rest of the New World. Best in autumn and winter, ripen at room temperature then store for a few days in the fridge.

figs

Figs, with their fragrant, swirly flesh, peak from late summer through to autumn, though some varieties actually fruit twice and are available both early and late in the season. Skin colour varies from green to purplish black and the flesh from white to pinkish brown. A gentle press is the best test for ripeness. A fig should have a little "give", but no bruising or soft spots. Figs ferment fast, so buy them close to when you want to eat them. Remove the stem and peel if the skin is thick. Store at room temperature in a single layer.

rhubarb

The stalks of rhubarb grow in a spectrum of colours from red to green and the leaves are bitter in flavour and poisonous if eaten in excess. Best in autumn and winter, look for varieties with large, healthy green leaves and deep red stalks, as they are likely to be the most flavoursome. Choose stalks that are flat and crisp, not curled or limp. Medium-sized stalks are generally less stringy than the larger ones. To maximise rhubarb's life, wrap unwashed stems tightly in plastic and store in the coolest part of the refrigerator.

fruit essentials

zesting + grating

Grated citrus rind and zest lend added depth to dishes because the rind contains highly fragrant oils. When a recipe calls for either, be sure to work gently on the surface of the fruit to remove only the rind, not the bitter white pith beneath it. Zest is removed with a tool that produces long fine shreds while rind can be grated with a coarse or finely toothed implement.

candied peel

Heat 3 cups (660g/1 lb 7 oz) sugar and 2 cups (500ml/16 fl oz) water in a saucepan over low heat, stirring until the sugar dissolves. Add the peel (with white pith removed) of three oranges and three lemons and simmer rapidly for 25 minutes. Brush down the sides of the pan occasionally with a pastry brush dipped in water. Remove from the heat and cool peel in the syrup. Citrus slices can also be poached in this syrup.

oxidisation

Oxidisation occurs when fruit such as apples or quinces are sliced and exposed to the air, making the white flesh turn brown very quickly. To avoid this, place the slices of fruit in a bowl of slightly acidulated water until just before serving. A generous squeeze of lemon juice or a crushed vitamin C tablet will provide the necessary amount of acid in the water.

peeling peaches + other stonefruit

Removing the skin results in peaches with a smooth, glossy surface and a lovely slippery texture. Place the peaches in a large saucepan of simmering water and simmer for 1 minute. Remove the peaches with a slotted spoon and place in a bowl of iced water for 5 minutes or until the skins start to wrinkle. Remove the skin by gently peeling it away with your fingers. Squeeze lemon juice over the peaches to prevent browning.

breakfasts + preserves

Rise and shine with a morning hit of big juicy berries, mouth-watering melons or luscious stone fruit. By keeping it simple you can make the most important meal of the day with minimum fuss yet maximum flavour impact. Prolong the pleasure of fruits in season by making jams and marmalade and your friends and family will appreciate your efforts for months to come.

fruit salad with lemongrass syrup, yoghurt and pistachios

mixed berry breakfast

banana fritters with maple syrup

fruit salad with lemongrass syrup, yoghurt and pistachios

2 stalks lemongrass, quartered
½ cup (110g/3¾ oz) caster (superfine) sugar
1 cup (250ml/8 fl oz) water
1 mango, sliced
½ rockmelon (cantaloupe), sliced
½ honeydew melon, sliced
1 nashi pear, sliced
¼ cup chopped raw pistachios
thick natural yoghurt, to serve

Place the lemongrass, sugar and water in a small saucepan over high heat. Bring to the boil and simmer for 5 minutes or until slightly thickened. Set syrup aside to cool. Top the fruit with the syrup and pistachios and serve with yoghurt. Serves 4.

mixed berry breakfast

2 cups frozen raspberries+
250g (8 oz) strawberries, halved
1 green apple, cored and sliced
½ cup (110g/3¾ oz) caster (superfine) sugar
1 cup (250g/8 oz) plain yoghurt
1 cup toasted muesli

Place the raspberries, strawberries, apple and sugar in a medium non-stick frying pan over high heat. Cook for 10 minutes or until the apple is tender, stirring constantly. Allow to cool completely. To serve, spoon the raspberry mixture into two glasses, top with the yoghurt and toasted muesli. Serves 4.
+ There is no need to defrost raspberries before use.
+ For a variation, use vanilla or berry-flavoured yoghurt instead of the plain yoghurt and replace the raspberries and strawberries with slices of skinned peach and nectarine.

banana fritters with maple syrup

2 cups (300g/10½ oz) plain (all-purpose) flour
3 teaspoons baking powder
⅔ cup (125g/4 oz) brown sugar
1 cup (250ml/8 fl oz) buttermilk
2 eggs
4 ripe bananas, mashed
20g (¾ oz) butter
2 bananas, extra, sliced lengthways, to serve
toasted flaked coconut, to serve
½ cup (125ml/4 fl oz) maple syrup

Place the flour, baking powder, sugar, buttermilk, eggs and bananas in a large bowl and mix to combine. Heat a large non-stick frying pan over medium heat. Add the butter and pour ⅓ cups (80ml/2½ fl oz) of the mixture into the pan and cook, in batches, until bubbles appear on the surface. Turn the fritters and cook for 1 minute or until golden. Repeat with the remaining mixture. Serve in stacks layered with the extra banana and topped with the coconut and maple syrup. Serves 4.

blueberry banana pancakes

2 cups (300g/10½ oz) plain (all-purpose) flour, sifted
3 teaspoons baking powder, sifted
½ cup (110g/3¾ oz) caster (superfine) sugar
1 egg
1¼ cups (310ml/10 fl oz) milk
¾ cup (185ml/6 fl oz) buttermilk
75g (2⅔ oz) butter, melted
blueberries and sliced bananas, to serve
maple syrup, to serve

Place the flour, baking powder and sugar in a bowl. Place the egg, milk, buttermilk and butter in a separate bowl and whisk until combined. Add the milk mixture to the flour mixture and whisk until smooth. Heat a greased medium non-stick frying pan over medium heat. Pour ⅓ cups (80ml/2½ fl oz) of the mixture into the pan and cook, in batches, until bubbles appear on the surface. Turn the pancakes and cook for 1 minute or until golden. Repeat with the remaining mixture. Serve in stacks with blueberries, bananas and maple syrup. Makes 15.

blueberry banana pancakes

nectarine French toast

nectarine granola

breakfast muffins

nectarine French toast

2 eggs
¼ cup (55g/1⅞ oz) caster (superfine) sugar
⅔ cup (165ml/5 fl oz) reduced-fat milk
⅓ cup (80g/2¾ oz) reduced-fat ricotta
2 tablespoons sugar
1 teaspoon vanilla extract
8 slices bread
4 nectarines, stoned and sliced
maple syrup, to serve

Place the eggs, caster sugar and milk in a medium bowl and whisk
to combine. Place the ricotta, sugar and vanilla in a small bowl and
stir to combine. Spread the ricotta mixture over 4 slices of bread.
Top with nectarine slices and the remaining bread. Place a large lightly
greased non-stick frying pan over medium heat. Dip the sandwiches
into the egg mixture and cook for 4–5 minutes each side or until golden.
Cut into wedges and serve with maple syrup. Serves 4.

nectarine granola

3 cups (300g/10½ oz) rolled oats
¼ cup raw pepitas (pumpkin seeds)
¼ cup sunflower seeds
¼ cup natural almonds, chopped
2 teaspoons ground cinnamon
½ cup (125ml/4 fl oz) honey
90ml (3 fl oz) canola oil
2 nectarines, stoned and sliced
2 cups (500g/1 lb) vanilla yoghurt

Preheat the oven to 180°C (350°F). Place the oats, pepitas, sunflower
seeds, almonds and cinnamon in a large bowl and mix to combine.
Stir the honey and oil in a small saucepan over low heat for 2 minutes
or until melted and combined. Add the honey mixture to the dry
ingredients and mix to combine. Divide the granola between two baking
trays lined with non-stick baking paper and spread evenly. Bake for
20–25 minutes, stirring occasionally, or until golden. Allow to cool
then divide toasted granola among serving glasses. Layer with slices
of nectarine and yoghurt. Serves 4

breakfast muffins

¾ cup (185ml/6 fl oz) vegetable oil
1½ cups (330g/11½ oz) caster (superfine) sugar
½ cup (125ml/4 fl oz) milk
3 eggs
3 cups (450g/15 oz) plain (all-purpose) flour, sifted
2 teaspoons baking powder
½ cup (50g/1¾ oz) rolled oats
1½ teaspoons cinnamon
1 apple, grated
2 bananas, mashed (¾ cup mashed banana)
250g strawberries, chopped (1½ cups chopped)
1 tablespoon raw sugar

Preheat the oven to 180°C (350°F). Place the oil, caster sugar, milk
and eggs in a medium bowl and whisk to combine. Place the flour,
baking powder, ⅓ cup of the oats and cinnamon in a large bowl and
stir to combine. Add the fruit to the flour mixture and stir to combine.
Add the milk mixture to the flour mixture and stir until just combined,
being careful not to overmix. Spoon into 12 x 1 cup (250ml/8 fl oz)
capacity lightly greased muffin tins. Sprinkle the tops with the remaining
oats and raw sugar. Bake for 25 minutes or until cooked when tested
with a skewer. Makes 12.

bircher muesli

1½ cups (150g/5¼ oz) rolled oats
1 cup (250ml/8 fl oz) apple juice, warmed
2 green apples, grated
1 cup (250g/8 oz) thick natural yoghurt
½ cup slivered almonds
honey, to serve

Place the oats and apple juice in a large bowl, cover with plastic wrap
and allow to stand for 30 minutes or until the oats are softened. Stir
in the grated apple. To serve, divide the yoghurt between 4 serving
glasses, top with the oat mixture, almonds and honey. Serves 4.

bircher muesli

blood orange marmalade

1kg (2 lb) blood oranges, washed
10 lemon seeds +
2¼ cups (495g/15⅞ oz) sugar
¼ cup (60ml/2 fl oz) lemon juice

Using a zester, zest the orange skins into thin strips and reserve.
Juice the oranges (you should have about 2 cups (500ml/16 fl oz)
of juice). Wrap the lemon seeds in a small piece of muslin and tie
to enclose. Place the orange zest and juice in a large deep frying
pan or jam pan with the sugar and lemon juice. Heat the pan over
medium–low heat, stirring until the sugar is dissolved. Add the muslin
bag of seeds and simmer for 30–35 minutes. Brush down the sides
of the pan occasionally with a pastry brush dipped in water. While
the jam is simmering, use a large metal spoon to skim any foam
from the surface. Place a saucer in the freezer to chill. To test
whether the marmalade is cooked, place a spoonful of marmalade
on the cold saucer then run your finger through it. If the line remains,
the marmalade is ready. If it doesn't, continue cooking and test
at 5-minute intervals. Remove the lemon seeds, then spoon the
marmalade into hot, sterilised jars (see glossary) and seal. Makes
approximately 4 cups. Store in the refrigerator for up to 6 months.
+ Lemon seeds are an essential part of this recipe because they
contain pectin, a setting agent, which helps set the marmalade.

strawberry jam

1.5kg (3 lb) strawberries
1kg (2¼ lb) sugar
¾ cup (185ml/6 fl oz) lime juice

Wash the strawberries well. Hull and slice in half. Place the strawberries,
sugar and lime juice in a jam pan or large deep frying pan. Bring to
the boil over medium heat, stirring until the sugar is dissolved. Simmer,
stirring occasionally, for 25–30 minutes or until thickened. While the
jam is simmering, use a large metal spoon to skim the foam from the
surface. Place a saucer in the freezer to chill. To test whether the jam
is ready, place a spoonful of jam on the cold saucer. Run your finger
through the jam. If the line remains, the jam is ready. If it doesn't,
continue cooking and test again at 5-minute intervals. Carefully pour
the hot jam into hot, sterilised jars (see glossary). Makes approximately
6 cups. Store in the refrigerator for up to 6 months.

blood orange marmalade

strawberry jam

rhubarb and vanilla preserve

250g (8 oz) rhubarb, trimmed and chopped
1 cup (220g/7¾ oz) sugar
1 vanilla bean, split, seeds scraped (or 1 teaspoon vanilla bean paste)
2 tablespoons water

Place the rhubarb, sugar, vanilla bean and seeds and water in a saucepan over low heat and stir until the sugar is dissolved. Increase the heat to medium and simmer for 8–10 minutes or until thickened. Remove the vanilla bean and discard. Spoon the jam into a hot, sterilised (see glossary) glass jar and seal. Makes approximately 1 cup. Store in the refrigerator for up to two weeks.

peach and passionfruit jam

1.4kg (2 lb 15 oz) yellow peaches
½ cup (125g/4 oz) passionfruit pulp
1kg (2¼ lb) sugar
¾ cup (185ml/6 fl oz) lime juice

Wash the peaches well. Remove the stones and slice the flesh. Place the peaches, passionfruit, sugar and lime juice in a jam pan or large deep frying pan. Bring to the boil over medium heat, stirring until the sugar is dissolved. Simmer, stirring occasionally, for 25–30 minutes or until thickened. While the jam is simmering, use a large metal spoon to skim the foam from the surface. Place a saucer in the freezer to chill. To test whether the jam is ready, place a spoonful of jam on the cold saucer. Run your finger through the jam. If the line remains, the jam is ready. If it doesn't, continue cooking and test the jam again at 5-minute intervals. Carefully pour the hot jam into hot, sterilised jars (see glossary). Makes approximately 8 cups. Store in the refrigerator for up to 6 months.

rhubarb and vanilla preserve   peach and passionfruit jam

desserts

The question of what to serve for dessert is never more appropriately answered than with a recipe based on perfectly ripe fruit. Keep it simple, let the fruit speak for itself and lend its luscious flavours and aromas to this collection, which includes traditional favourites with a twist as well as contemporary treats. Simply serve and stand back as there's bound to be a rush for seconds.

poached summer fruits

lemon soufflé

summer trifle

poached summer fruits

2 cups (500ml/16 fl oz) water
1 cup (220g/7¾ oz) sugar
1 vanilla bean, split and seeds scraped
4 peaches, peeled (method, page 17)
4 nectarines, peeled (method, page 17)
4 apricots, peeled (method, page 17)
2⅔ cups raspberries
2⅔ cups blueberries

Place the water, sugar and vanilla bean and seeds in a medium saucepan over medium heat and stir until the sugar is dissolved. Simmer until the liquid is reduced by half. Pour the hot syrup over the peeled fruit and allow to cool. To serve, toss the raspberries and blueberries through the stone fruit and place in bowls. Remove the vanilla bean and spoon over the syrup. Serves 4.

lemon soufflé

⅔ cup (150g/5¼ oz) caster (superfine) sugar
2 tablespoons water
2 teaspoons cornflour (cornstarch)
100ml (3½ fl oz) lemon juice
5 egg whites
1½ tablespoons caster (superfine) sugar, extra
50g (1¾ oz) butter, melted
caster (superfine) sugar, extra, for dusting

Preheat the oven to 180°C (350°F). Place the sugar and water in a small saucepan over low heat. Stir until the sugar is dissolved, brushing down any sugar crystals from the sides of the pan. Mix the cornflour and juice in a small bowl until dissolved, then add to the sugar syrup. Increase the heat and bring to the boil, stirring until slightly thickened. Remove from the heat and cool slightly. Place the egg whites in the bowl of an electric mixer and whisk until soft peaks form. Gradually add the extra sugar and whisk until stiff peaks form. Fold in the lemon syrup. Brush 4 x 1¼ cup (310ml/10 fl oz) capacity straight-sided dishes with butter and dust with the extra sugar. Spoon the mixture into the dishes until three-quarters full, place on a baking tray and bake for 12 minutes or until risen and golden. Makes 4.

summer trifle

1 cup (250ml/8 fl oz) dessert wine
⅓ cup (75g/2⅔ oz) sugar
1 peach, stoned and thinly sliced
1 nectarine, plum or apricot, stoned and thinly sliced
20cm (8 in) square store-bought sponge cake (or see recipe, page 89)
raspberry cream
1 cup (250ml/8 fl oz) (single or pouring) cream
150g (5¼ oz) fresh or frozen raspberries +
1 tablespoon icing (confectioner's) sugar, sifted

Place the wine and sugar in a saucepan over low heat and stir until the sugar is dissolved. Increase the heat and simmer for 5 minutes or until syrupy. Set aside to cool. Place the fruit in a bowl and pour over just enough syrup to coat the fruit slices. Cut the cake into 8 thick slices and place half on plates. Spoon over half of the remaining syrup to soak the cake.

To make the raspberry cream, place the cream in a chilled bowl and beat until soft peaks form. Lightly crush the raspberries with a fork and fold through the cream with the icing sugar. Spoon half of the raspberry cream over the sponge pieces and top with half of the fruit. Repeat the layers with the remaining sponge cake, syrup, raspberry cream and fruit and serve immediately. Serves 4.

+ If using frozen raspberries there is no need to defrost them first.

berries and figs in vanilla syrup

1 cup (250ml/8 fl oz) water
½ cup (110g/3¾ oz) sugar
1 vanilla bean, split and seeds scraped
120g (3⅞ oz) raspberries
150g (5¼ oz) blueberries
250g (8 oz) strawberries
4 figs, halved

Place the water, sugar and vanilla bean and seeds in a small saucepan and stir over low heat until the sugar is dissolved. Increase the heat and boil for 5 minutes. Remove from the heat and allow to cool. Pour the syrup over the combined berries and figs. Serves 4.

+ Serve this combination with ice-cream or heavy or double cream.

berries and figs in vanilla syrup

fruit sorbet

fruit galettes

peach and vanilla panna cotta

fruit sorbet

¾ cup (165g/5¾ oz) caster (superfine) sugar
1 cup (250ml/8 fl oz) water
1¾ cups strained raspberry puree (from approx 700g/24 oz fresh
  or frozen berries)
¼ cup (60ml/2 fl oz) lime juice

Place the sugar and water in a saucepan over low heat and stir without boiling until the sugar is dissolved. Increase the heat and bring to the boil for 1 minute. Set aside to cool. Combine the raspberry puree, lime juice and the sugar syrup, place in an ice-cream maker and follow the manufacturer's instructions to freeze. Serves 4–6.
+ To make mango sorbet, replace the strained raspberry puree with 4 mangoes, peeled, stoned and pureed (approximately 1kg/2 lb chopped mango) and increase the lime juice to ½ cup (125ml/4 fl oz).

fruit galettes

375g (13¼ oz) block store-bought puff pastry, thawed
ripe fruit in season, very thinly sliced
caster (superfine) sugar, for sprinkling

Preheat the oven to 200°C (400°F). Roll out pastry on a lightly floured surface until 3mm (⅛ in) thick. Cut into 8 rectangles and place on baking trays lined with non-stick baking paper. Top with the fruit slices. Sprinkle with sugar and bake for 20 minutes or until golden. Makes 8.
+ Serve fruit galettes for breakfast or brunch; or with heavy or double cream or ice-cream for dessert.

peach and vanilla panna cotta

1½ cups (375ml/12 fl oz) water
½ cup (110g/3¾ oz) sugar
3 peaches, halved and stoned
1 tablespoon powdered gelatine
1 quantity panna cotta (recipe, page 89)

Place the water and sugar in a medium saucepan over medium heat and stir until the sugar is dissolved. Add the peaches and simmer for 3–5 minutes or until soft. Remove the peaches (reserving the poaching liquid), slip off the skins and set the fruit aside. Place ¼ cup (125ml/ 4 fl oz) of the poaching liquid in a bowl, sprinkle over the gelatine and set aside for 5 minutes. Add the gelatine mixture to the remaining liquid in the saucepan, stir through and simmer until dissolved. Place peaches, cut-side up, in a greased 26 x 8 x 7.5cm (10 x 3¼ x 3 in) loaf tin and pour over the liquid. Refrigerate for 2 hours or until firm. Pour the panna cotta over the set jelly and refrigerate for 6 hours. Dip the tin in warm water and invert onto a plate. Serves 6.

raspberry semifreddo

3 eggs
2 egg yolks, extra
½ teaspoon vanilla extract
1 cup (225g/8 oz) caster (superfine) sugar
500g (1 lb) frozen raspberries
1¾ cups (435ml/14 fl oz) (single or pouring) cream

Place the eggs, egg yolks, vanilla and sugar in a heatproof bowl. Place over a saucepan of simmering water and whisk the mixture with a hand-held beater for 4–5 minutes or until heated, thick and pale. Remove from the heat and whisk until cool. Lightly crush or break up the raspberries and gently fold through the egg mixture. Set aside. Place the cream in the bowl of an electric mixer and whisk until soft peaks form. Gently fold the egg mixture into the cream until just combined. Wrap pieces of non-stick baking paper around 6 x 1 cup (250ml/8 fl oz) capacity serving glasses, making sure the paper stands at least 1cm (½ in) above the rim. Secure with sticky tape. Spoon the mixture into glasses and freeze for 4–6 hours or until firm. Remove the paper to serve. Serves 6.

raspberry semifreddo

strawberry ice-cream

1kg (2 lb) strawberries, pureed and strained (3 cups/750ml/24 fl oz)
½ cup (110g/3¾ oz) caster (superfine) sugar
1 cup (250ml/8 fl oz) milk
2 cups (500ml/16 fl oz) (pouring or single) cream
6 egg yolks
⅔ cup (150g/5¼ oz) caster (superfine) sugar, extra

Stir the strawberry puree and sugar in a small saucepan over low heat until the sugar is dissolved. Increase the heat and boil, stirring occasionally, for 10–12 minutes or until reduced to 1¾ cups (435ml/14 fl oz). Remove from the heat and set aside to cool. Heat the milk and cream in a saucepan over medium heat until hot (but not boiling). Remove from the heat. Place the egg yolks and the extra sugar in a bowl and whisk until thick and pale. Slowly pour the hot cream mixture into the egg yolk mixture, whisking continuously. Pour the mixture back into the saucepan and stir over low heat for 4 minutes or until it is slightly thickened and just coats the back of a spoon. Set aside to cool. Pour the cooled custard into an ice-cream maker and follow the manufacturer's instructions until the ice-cream is just firm. Add the strawberry puree and churn for 1–2 minutes or until combined. Alternatively, see glossary for the still-freezing method. Makes 5½ cups (1.4 litres/44 fl oz).

pavlova

4 (150ml/4¾ fl oz) egg whites
1 cup (220g/7¾ oz) caster (superfine) sugar
3 teaspoons cornflour (cornstarch)
1 teaspoon white vinegar
whipped cream, to serve
fresh fruit, to serve

Preheat the oven to 150°C (300°F). Place the egg whites in the bowl of an electric mixer and beat until soft peaks form. Gradually add the sugar, beating well until the mixture is glossy. Sift the cornflour over the egg white mixture and fold through with the vinegar. Pile the meringue mixture into an 18cm (7 in) round on a baking tray lined with non-stick baking paper. Place in the oven, reduce the temperature to 120°C (250°F) and cook for 1 hour. Turn the oven off and allow the meringue to cool in the oven. Top with whipped cream and fresh fruit and serve immediately. Serves 6–8.

strawberry ice-cream

pavlova

rhubarb and vanilla crumble   teacup banana puddings

classic poached pears

rhubarb and vanilla crumble

850g (1¾ lb) rhubarb, trimmed and chopped
⅔ cup (165g/5¼ oz) demerara sugar
1 vanilla bean, split and seeds scraped
crumble topping
1 cup (150g/5¼ oz) plain (all-purpose) flour
⅓ cup (75g/2⅔ oz) sugar
100g (3½ oz) butter

Preheat the oven to 180°C (350°F). Combine the rhubarb, sugar and vanilla bean and seeds. Place in a 6 cup (1.5 litre/48 fl oz) capacity ovenproof dish. To make the topping, combine the flour, sugar and butter. Pile the mixture on top of the fruit. Bake for 50 minutes or until the topping is golden and the rhubarb is soft. Serves 4.

teacup banana puddings

20g (¾ oz) butter
1 cup (175g/6 oz) brown sugar
¼ cup (60ml/2 fl oz) water
2 bananas, thinly sliced
⅔ cup (75g/2⅔ oz) almond meal (ground almonds)
½ cup (75g/2⅔ oz) plain (all-purpose) flour
1 cup (150g/5¼ oz) icing (confectioner's) sugar
¼ teaspoon baking powder
3 egg whites
1 teaspoon vanilla extract
75g (2⅔ oz) butter, extra, melted

Place the butter, sugar and water in a small saucepan over low heat and stir until the sugar is dissolved. Bring to the boil and cook for 3–4 minutes or until the sauce is syrupy. Set aside. Place slices of the banana in 4 x 1 cup (250ml/8 fl oz) capacity greased ovenproof teacups. Spoon half the sauce over the bananas, place the teacups on a baking tray. Set aside. Preheat the oven to 180°C (350°F). Sift the almond meal, flour, icing sugar and baking powder into a bowl and stir to combine. Add the egg whites, vanilla and extra butter and stir to combine. Spoon the mixture over the bananas and bake for 20 minutes or until golden and cooked when tested with a skewer. Invert the puddings onto plates and serve with the remaining sauce. Makes 4.

classic poached pears

2 cups (500ml/16 fl oz) red wine
2 cups (500ml/16 fl oz) water
¾ cup (165g/5¾ oz) sugar
1 cinnamon stick
1 clove
2 x 5cm (2 in) pieces orange rind
6 brown pears, peeled

Place the wine, water, sugar, cinnamon, clove and orange rind in a saucepan. Heat, stirring, over medium–low heat until the sugar is dissolved. Simmer for 5 minutes, add the pears and cover. Simmer slowly for 30 minutes, turning the pears occasionally. Remove from the heat. Serve the pears with a little of the poaching liquid. Serves 6.

crème brûlée with passionfruit topping

4 cups (1 litre/32 fl oz) (single or pouring) cream
2 vanilla beans, split and seeds scraped
8 egg yolks
½ cup (110g/3¾ oz) caster (superfine) sugar
¾ cup (165g/5¾ oz) caster (superfine) sugar, extra
pulp of 1 passionfruit

Preheat the oven to 160°C (320°F). Place the cream and vanilla bean and seeds in a saucepan over low heat and cook gently until the mixture just comes to the boil. Remove from the heat and discard the beans. Whisk the egg yolks and sugar together until thick and pale. Pour the warm cream mixture over the egg mixture and whisk to combine. Return the mixture to the saucepan and stir over low heat for 6–8 minutes or until the custard coats the back of a spoon. Pour the custard into 8 x ½ cup (125ml/4 fl oz) capacity ovenproof dishes and place in a deep baking dish, add boiling water to come halfway up the sides of the dishes. Bake for 25 minutes or until just set. Refrigerate for 3 hours or until the custard is completely set. Combine the extra sugar and passionfruit pulp. Cover the brûlées with the passionfruit sugar and caramelise the sugar with a blowtorch or heated spoon (see glossary). Serves 8.

crème brûlée with passionfruit topping

raspberry and rosé jelly

¾ cup (185ml/6 fl oz) rosé wine
¾ cup (185ml/6 fl oz) water
⅓ cup (75g/2⅔ oz) caster (superfine) sugar
2 teaspoons powdered gelatine
⅓ cup raspberries
vanilla cream
½ cup (125ml/4 fl oz) (single or pouring) cream
2 tablespoons caster (superfine) sugar
½ vanilla bean, split, seeds scraped

Place the wine, ½ cup (125ml/4 fl oz) of the water and the sugar in a small saucepan over medium heat and bring to the boil. Remove from the heat. Place the remaining water and gelatine in a bowl and stir. Add to the wine mixture and stir until dissolved. Place the raspberries in 2 x 1 cup (250ml/8 fl oz) capacity glasses. Pour over enough wine mixture to just cover the berries and refrigerate until set. Divide the remaining wine mixture between the glasses and refrigerate until set.

To make the vanilla cream, place the cream, sugar and vanilla seeds in a bowl and whisk until soft peaks form. Top the jelly with the vanilla cream to serve. Makes 2.

passionfruit soufflé

⅔ cup (150g/5¼ oz) caster (superfine) sugar
2 tablespoons water
2 teaspoons cornflour (cornstarch)
100ml (3½ fl oz) passionfruit pulp
5 egg whites
1½ tablespoons caster (superfine) sugar, extra
50g (1¾ oz) butter, melted
caster (superfine) sugar, extra, for dusting

Preheat the oven to 180°C (350°F). Place the sugar and water in a small saucepan over low heat. Stir until the sugar is dissolved, brushing down any sugar crystals from the sides of the pan. Mix the cornflour and passionfruit pulp in a cup or small bowl until the cornflour is dissolved, then add to the sugar syrup. Increase the heat and bring to the boil, stirring until slightly thickened. Remove from the heat and cool slightly. Place the egg whites in the bowl of an electric mixer and whisk until soft peaks form. Gradually add the extra sugar and whisk until stiff peaks form. Fold through the passionfruit sugar syrup. Brush 4 x 1½ cup (375ml/12 fl oz) capacity straight-sided dishes with the butter and dust with the extra sugar. Spoon the soufflé mixture into the dishes until ¾ full, place on a baking tray and cook for 12 minutes or until risen and golden. Makes 4.

raspberry and rosé jelly   passionfruit soufflé

pies + tarts

A straw poll of the donna hay kitchen reveals that our
absolute favourite comfort food is anything involving
pastry. And when that pastry is matched with the season's
best fruit everyone clamours for more. Team with the pie
and tart's greatest ally, a scoop of ice-cream or a delicious
dollop of cream or mascarpone, and the journey to deep
contentment will be complete.

rustic peach and plum pie

pineapple tarte tatin

individual rhubarb crumble tarts

rustic peach and plum pie

1 quantity sweet shortcrust pastry (recipe, page 90)
¼ cup (30g/1 oz) almond meal (ground almonds)
4 ripe peaches, stoned and cut into wedges
4 plums, stoned and cut into wedges
1 tablespoon sugar

Preheat the oven to 180°C (350°F). Roll out the pastry on a lightly floured surface into a rough circle 3mm (⅛ in) thick and place on a baking tray lined with non-stick baking paper. Sprinkle the pastry with the almond meal, leaving a 5cm (2 in) border. Place the peach and plum wedges on top and sprinkle the sugar over. Fold the sides of the pastry up to partially enclose the fruit. Refrigerate for 10 minutes. Bake for 45 minutes or until golden brown. Serves 6–8.

pineapple tarte tatin

60g (2 oz) butter
1 cup (220g/7¾ oz) caster (superfine) sugar
¼ cup (60ml/2 fl oz) water
1 small pineapple, peeled and sliced
375g (13¼ oz) block store-bought puff pastry, thawed

Preheat the oven to 200°C (400°F). Place a non-stick frying pan over medium heat. Add the butter and allow to melt. Add the sugar and water and cook, stirring, for 2 minutes or until the sugar is dissolved. Add the pineapple and cook for 3 minutes. Place a pineapple slice and a little of the syrup in the bases of 6 x 9cm (3½ in) pie tins. Roll out the pastry on a lightly floured surface until 3mm (⅛ in) thick. Cut out 6 x 9cm (3½ in) rounds of pastry and place over the pineapple, tucking under the edges. Place the tins on a baking tray and bake for 18–20 minutes or until puffed and golden. To serve, invert the tarte tatins onto plates. Makes 6.

individual rhubarb crumble tarts

1 x 200g (7 oz) sheet store-bought shortcrust pastry, thawed
200g (7 oz) rhubarb, trimmed
3 tablespoons brown sugar
30g (1 oz) store-bought biscotti, crushed
1 egg, lightly beaten

Preheat the oven to 200°C (400°F). Cut out 4 x 12cm (4¾ in) squares from the pastry. Place on a baking tray lined with non-stick baking paper. Cut the rhubarb into 12cm (4¾ in) lengths. Place the rhubarb and sugar in a bowl and toss to combine. Divide the crushed biscotti between the pastry squares and top with the rhubarb. Brush the edges of the pastry with the egg. Bake for 15 minutes or until the pastry is golden and the rhubarb is soft. Serves 4.

crushed raspberry tart

375g (13¼ oz) block store-bought puff pastry, thawed
1 egg white, lightly beaten
1 tablespoon caster (superfine) sugar
2 cups (250g/8 oz) raspberries
1 tablespoon icing (confectioner's) sugar, sifted
sour cream filling
1 cup (250g/8 oz) sour cream
¼ cup (60ml/2 fl oz) (single or pouring) cream
⅓ cup (60g/2 oz) brown sugar

Preheat the oven to 200°C (400°F). Roll out the pastry on a lightly floured surface to 3mm (⅛ in) thickness and trim to a 20cm (8 in) square. Cut 8 strips measuring 1 x 20cm (½ x 8 in) from the remaining pastry. Place the pastry square on a baking tray lined with non-stick baking paper. Brush with the egg white and place half the strips around the edge to form a border. Brush the borders with the egg white and place the remaining strips on top. Prick the base with a fork. Cover and refrigerate for 30 minutes. Sprinkle the pastry with the caster sugar. Bake for 20 minutes or until golden. To make the sour cream filling, whisk the sour cream, cream and brown sugar in a bowl until smooth. Combine half the raspberries with the icing sugar and crush lightly. Fold in the remaining raspberries. Spread the sour cream filling over the pastry base and spoon over the raspberries. Serves 6.

crushed raspberry tart

lemon tart

quince tarte tatin

cinnamon pear pies

lemon tart

1 quantity sweet shortcrust pastry (recipe, page 90)
¾ cup (185ml/6 fl oz) lemon juice
¾ cup (165g/5¾ oz) caster (superfine) sugar
¾ cup (185ml/6 fl oz) (single or pouring) cream
3 eggs, lightly beaten

Preheat the oven to 180°C (350°F). Roll out the pastry on a lightly floured surface to 3mm (⅛ in) thickness. Place in a lightly greased 22cm (8½ in) fluted, removable-base tart tin. Trim the edge, line the pastry with non-stick baking paper and fill with pastry weights or uncooked rice or beans. Bake for 10 minutes, remove the weights and bake for a further 10 minutes or until the pastry is golden. Reduce the oven temperature to 140°C (280°F). Place the lemon juice and sugar in a heatproof bowl over a saucepan of simmering water and stir until the sugar is dissolved. Add the cream and eggs and stir continuously for 5 minutes. Strain the egg mixture into the tart shell and bake for 20–25 minutes or until the filling is almost set. Cool. Serves 8.

quince tarte tatin

3 quinces, peeled and cored
2 cups (500ml/16 fl oz) water
1 cup (220g/7¾ oz) sugar
4 pieces lemon peel
80g (2¾ oz) butter, divided into 4 pieces
375g (13¼ oz) block store-bought puff pastry, thawed

Cut the quinces into 2cm (1 in) slices. Heat a large frying pan over medium to high heat. Add the quinces, water, sugar and peel, cover and cook for 45 minutes or until the quinces are ruby-coloured and soft. Simmer the quinces, uncovered, for 10 minutes to reduce the syrup. Remove the lemon peel and divide the quinces and their pan juices among 4 x 14cm (5½ in) frying pans. Top each with a piece of butter. (Or you can use a 25cm (10 in) pan.)

  Preheat the oven to 200°C (400°F). Roll out the pastry on a lightly floured surface to 3mm (⅛ in) thickness. Cut into 4 and place over the quinces to cover the top of the pans. Tuck in the pastry edges to neaten. Bake for 15–20 minutes (35 minutes for the large pan) or until the pastry is golden. To serve, turn out onto plates. Serves 4.

cinnamon pear pies

4 firm pears, peeled, with stems intact
1 cup (220g/7¾ oz) sugar
2 cinnamon sticks
4 cups (1 litre/32 fl oz) water
almond filling
¾ cup (165g/5¾ oz) caster (superfine) sugar
40g (1½ oz) butter, softened
½ teaspoon vanilla extract
¾ cup (185ml/6 fl oz) (single or pouring) cream
2 eggs, separated
1 cup (110g/3¾ oz) almond meal (ground almonds)
¼ cup (40g/1½ oz) self-raising (self-rising) flour, sifted

Place the pears, sugar, cinnamon and water in a saucepan. Cover and simmer over low heat for 15–20 minutes or until the pears are just soft. Allow to cool. Preheat the oven to 180°C (350°F).

  To make almond filling, place sugar, butter, vanilla, cream, egg yolks, almond meal and flour in the bowl of an electric mixer and beat until thick. Place egg whites in a bowl and beat until soft peaks form, fold into the almond mixture and spoon into 4 x 1½ cup (375ml/12 fl oz) ovenproof dishes. Press a pear into each and bake for 30 minutes or until filling is firm. Serves 4.

mango and almond tart

2 x 200g (7 oz) sheets store-bought puff pastry, thawed
1 egg, lightly beaten
¼ cup (30g/1 oz) almond meal (ground almonds)
⅓ cup (60g/2 oz) brown sugar
3 mangoes, peeled, cheeks removed and halved

Preheat the oven to 200°C (400°F). Brush the edge of one sheet of pastry with egg. Place another sheet of puff pastry slightly overlapping, join the edges with the other pastry to form a rectangle and place on a baking tray lined with non-stick baking paper. Cut 1cm (½ in) from the edges of the pastry sheet and place around the edges to form a border. Sprinkle the pastry with the almond meal and 1 tablespoon of the brown sugar. Top with the mangoes and sprinkle with the remaining brown sugar. Bake for 30 minutes or until pastry is golden. Serves 12.

mango and almond tart

blistered plum and mascarpone tart

6 plums, halved and stones removed

¼ cup (55g/1⅞ oz) caster (superfine) sugar

2 sheets store-bought puff pastry, thawed

1 egg yolk, lightly beaten

brandy syrup

1 cup (250ml/8 fl oz) water

2 tablespoons brandy

1 cup (220g/7¾ oz) caster (superfine) sugar

vanilla mascarpone filling

1 cup (250g/8 oz) mascarpone cheese

2 teaspoons icing (confectioner's) sugar

1 vanilla bean, split and seeds scraped

Heat a non-stick frying pan over medium high heat. Sprinkle the plums with the sugar and cook cut-side down for 1–2 minutes or until the sugar is melted and golden. Set aside.

To make the brandy syrup, place the water, brandy and sugar in a small saucepan over high heat and bring to the boil. Reduce the heat to low and simmer for 12–15 minutes or until the mixture thickens. Set aside and allow to cool.

To make the vanilla mascarpone filling, place the mascarpone, icing sugar and vanilla seeds in a bowl and whisk to combine. Set aside.

Preheat the oven to 200°C (400°F). Cut out 4 x 12cm (4¾ in) squares from one sheet of pastry and place on a baking tray lined with baking paper. Brush with the egg. Cut 16 x 1cm (½ in) wide strips from the other sheet of pastry. Place the strips around the pastry squares to form the borders, trim the edges and brush with remaining egg. Bake for 10–12 minutes or until puffed and golden. Spoon the vanilla filling into the tarts and top with the plums. Serve with the brandy syrup. Serves 4.

caramelised apple tart

60g (2 oz) butter

¾ cup (165g/5¾ oz) caster (superfine) sugar

2 tablespoons water

4 apples, peeled, cored and quartered

375g (13¼ oz) block store-bought puff pastry, thawed

Preheat the oven to 200°C (400°F). Place an 18cm (7 in) frying pan with an ovenproof handle over medium heat. Add the butter and allow to melt. Add the sugar and water and cook, stirring, for 2 minutes or until the sugar is dissolved. Continue to cook for 5 minutes or until golden and syrupy. Add the apples to the pan and cook for 5 minutes. Allow the bubbles to subside then arrange the apple pieces in a circular pattern, core-side up, over the base of the frying pan. Roll out the pastry on a lightly floured surface to 3mm (⅛ in) thickness. Cut out a 24cm (9½ in) circle and place over the apples, tucking the edge under. Bake for 18–20 minutes or until the pastry is puffed and golden. To serve, invert the tart onto a plate. Serves 4–6.

blistered plum and mascarpone tart

caramelised apple tart

blood orange tart   fig tarts with brown sugar mascarpone

apple pie

blood orange tart

1 quantity sweet shortcrust pastry (recipe, page 90)
blood orange filling
½ cup (110g/3¾ oz) caster (superfine) sugar
¾ cup (185ml/6 fl oz) blood orange juice, strained
¼ cup (60ml/2 fl oz) lemon juice
4 eggs
1 egg yolk, extra
1 cup (250ml/8 fl oz) (single or pouring) cream
1 tablespoon finely grated blood orange rind

Preheat the oven to 180°C (350°F). Roll out the pastry on a lightly floured surface to 3mm (⅛ in) thickness and line a 22cm (8½ in) tart tin. Trim the pastry and refrigerate for 10 minutes. Line the pastry with non-stick baking paper and fill with baking weights or uncooked rice. Bake for 10–12 minutes, remove the weights and bake for a further 10 minutes or until light golden brown. Remove and set aside. Reduce the oven temperature to 140°C (285°F).

To make the filling, place the sugar, orange juice and lemon juice in a heatproof bowl over a saucepan of simmering water. Stir until the sugar is dissolved. Add the eggs, egg yolk, cream and orange rind, stir for 5 minutes and pour into the tart shell. Bake for 30 minutes or until the filling is just set. Cool, then refrigerate until firm. Top with candied orange slices and syrup (recipe, page 16). Serves 8–10.

fig tarts with brown sugar mascarpone

1 x 200g (7 oz) sheet store-bought butter puff pastry, thawed
2 teaspoons caster (superfine) sugar
4 figs, quartered
2 teaspoons brown sugar
25g (⅞ oz) butter, chopped
1 cup (250g/8 fl oz) mascarpone cheese
2 tablespoons brown sugar, extra

Preheat the oven to 200°C (400°F). Cut pastry into 4 rectangles and place on a baking tray lined with non-stick baking paper. Sprinkle with the caster sugar and top with the figs. Sprinkle over the brown sugar and butter. Bake for 15 minutes or until the pastry is puffed. Serve with the mascarpone sprinkled with extra brown sugar. Serves 4.

apple pie

1 quantity sweet shortcrust pastry (recipe, page 90)
2 tablespoons almond meal (ground almonds)
1 egg, lightly beaten
sugar, for sprinkling
apple filling
8 green apples, peeled and chopped
1 tablespoon water
⅓ cup (75g/2⅔ oz) sugar
1 tablespoon lemon juice
½ teaspoon ground cinnamon

Preheat the oven to 190°C (375°F). To make the filling, place the apples and water in a deep frying pan over medium heat. Cover and simmer, shaking the pan occasionally, for 5 minutes or until just tender. Drain and cool completely. Stir in the sugar, lemon juice and cinnamon. Roll ⅔ of the pastry on a floured surface to 3mm (⅛ in) thickness and place in a shallow 24cm (9½ in) pie tin. Sprinkle over the almond meal and pack the apples tightly into the pastry shell. Roll out the remaining pastry to fit over the top of the pie. Brush the rim with water, press the edges together and trim. Cut slits in the top, brush with the egg and sprinkle with sugar. Bake for 30 minutes or until the pastry is golden and crisp. Serves 8.

free-form rhubarb and blackcurrant pies

400g (14 oz) rhubarb, trimmed and chopped
⅓ cup blackcurrants
1 cup (220g/7¾ oz) caster (superfine) sugar
2 tablespoons cornflour (cornstarch)
4 sheets store-bought shortcrust pastry, thawed
1 egg, lightly beaten
1 tablespoon caster (superfine) sugar, extra

Preheat the oven to 200°C (400°F). Toss the rhubarb, blackcurrants, sugar and cornflour in a bowl. Use a 19cm (7½ in) cutter to cut out a circle from each pastry sheet. Divide the rhubarb mixture between the circles and bring the edges of the pastry together to partially enclose the rhubarb. Brush the pastry with the egg and sprinkle with the extra sugar. Bake for 15–20 minutes or until the pastry is golden. Makes 4.

free-form rhubarb and blackcurrant pies

apricot turnovers

375g (13¼ oz) block store-bought puff pastry, thawed
1 x 825g (29 oz) can apricot halves, drained
milk, for brushing
sugar, for sprinkling

Preheat the oven to 200°C (400°F). Roll out the pastry on a lightly floured surface to 3mm (⅛ in) thickness, cut into 6 x 11cm (4½ in) circles and place on a baking tray lined with non-stick baking paper. Divide the apricots between the circles, placing them on one half of each round. Sprinkle with the sugar, brush the edges with the milk, fold over and fork the edges together. Brush with milk, sprinkle with sugar and bake for 25 minutes or until golden. Makes 4.

almond pear tart

1 quantity sweet shortcrust pastry (recipe, page 90)
poached pears
3 cups (750ml/24 fl oz) water
1½ cups (330g/11½ oz) sugar
3 brown pears, peeled, halved and cored, stems intact
almond filling
75g (2⅔ oz) butter
½ cup (110g/3¾ oz) caster (superfine) sugar
1 egg
1⅓ cups (150g/5¼ oz) almond meal (ground almonds)
2 tablespoons plain (all-purpose) flour
1½ tablespoons brandy

Preheat the oven to 180°C (350°F). Roll out the pastry between sheets of non-stick baking paper to 3mm (⅛ in) thickness and line a lightly greased 22cm (9 in) tart ring. Trim the edge, line the pastry with non-stick baking paper and fill with baking weights or uncooked rice. Bake for 10–12 minutes, remove the weights and paper and bake for a further 10 minutes or until light golden brown. Cool.

To make the poached pears, place the water and sugar in a saucepan over medium–low heat. Stir until the sugar is dissolved, then simmer for 5 minutes. Add the pears and simmer for 15 minutes or until tender. Remove from the saucepan and cool on absorbent paper.

To make the almond filling, place the butter and sugar in a bowl and beat with an electric hand mixer until light and creamy. Beat in the egg, then fold in the almond meal, flour and brandy. Spread the filling over the pastry. Slice the pears, keeping the stems intact, and arrange them over the filling. Bake the tart for 50 minutes or until golden. Serve at room temperature. Serves 6.

apricot turnovers

almond pear tart

cakes + bakes

Baking fruit releases the sweet juices and intensifies the flavour, so prepare for sensory overload with this selection of cakes, slices, muffins and other baked goodies. The beauty of baking is that after the initial preparation you pretty much leave the oven to do the work. That means you're free to kick back and enjoy some quiet downtime or the company of family and friends.

lemon cake with passionfruit syrup

simple peach and almond cakes

berry and brioche bake

lemon cake with passionfruit syrup

125g (4 oz) butter, softened

1 cup (220g/7¾ oz) caster (superfine) sugar

2 eggs

1 cup (250g/8 oz) sour cream

¼ cup (60ml/2 fl oz) lemon juice

1 tablespoon finely grated lemon rind

2½ cups (300g/10½ oz) self-raising (self-rising) flour

½ teaspoon baking powder

passionfruit syrup

⅔ cup (165ml/5 fl oz) passionfruit pulp

⅔ cup (150g/5¼ oz) caster (superfine) sugar

1 cup (250ml/8 fl oz) water

Preheat the oven to 180°C (350°F). Place the butter and caster sugar in the bowl of an electric mixer and beat until light and creamy. Add the eggs and beat well. Mix through the sour cream, lemon juice, rind, flour and baking powder. Spoon the mixture into a lightly greased 23cm (9 in) round cake tin lined with non-stick baking paper. Bake for 40 minutes or until cooked when tested with a skewer. Leave the cake in the tin for 5 minutes then place on a rack over a plate.

To make the passionfruit syrup, place the passionfruit, sugar and water in a saucepan. Cook over low heat, stirring, until the sugar is dissolved, then increase the heat and boil the syrup for 4–5 minutes or until it thickens slightly. Pour half the hot syrup over the top of the hot cake. Allow the cake to stand for 5 minutes then serve with the remaining syrup. Serves 8–10.

simple peach and almond cakes

1 cup (250ml/8 fl oz) (single or pouring) cream

1 teaspoon icing (confectioner's) sugar

1 teaspoon vanilla extract

4 small store-bought almond or sponge cakes

2 peaches, stones removed and sliced

¼ cup (60ml/2 fl oz) passionfruit pulp

Place the cream, sugar and vanilla in a bowl and whisk until soft peaks form. Place the almond cakes on plates and top with the cream mixture, peach slices and passionfruit pulp. Serves 4.

berry and brioche bake

1 tablespoon butter, for greasing

1 tablespoon sugar

1 loaf brioche (see glossary), thickly sliced

500g (1 lb) strawberries, halved

150g (5¼ oz) blueberries

⅓ cup (80ml/2½ fl oz) muscat

3 tablespoons sugar, extra

Preheat the oven to 180°C (350°F). Grease a 23 x 18cm (9 x 7 in) baking dish with the butter and sprinkle the sugar over the base. Top with the brioche slices. Combine the strawberries, blueberries, muscat and extra sugar in a medium bowl. Spoon the berry mixture over the brioche and bake for 35 minutes or until the berries are soft and the brioche is golden. Serves 8.

orange and poppy seed cake

250g (8 oz) butter, softened

1 cup (220g/7¾ oz) caster (superfine) sugar

3 eggs

¼ cup poppy seeds

1 tablespoon finely grated orange rind

½ cup (125ml/4 fl oz) milk

2 cups (300g/10½ oz) self-raising (self-rising) flour, sifted

orange syrup

1 cup (220g/7¾ oz) caster (superfine) sugar

1 cup (250ml/8 fl oz) freshly squeezed orange juice

½ cup orange zest

Preheat the oven to 160°C (325°F). Place the butter and sugar in the bowl of an electric mixer and beat until light and creamy. Gradually add the eggs and beat well. Add the poppy seeds, orange rind, milk and flour and stir to combine. Spoon the mixture into a lightly greased 22cm (8½ in) square cake tin lined with non-stick baking paper. Bake for 55 minutes or until cooked when tested with a skewer.

To make the orange syrup, place the sugar, orange juice and zest in a small saucepan over low heat and stir until the sugar is dissolved. Increase the heat and boil for 7–8 minutes or until syrupy. To serve pour the syrup over the cake. Serves 10.

orange and poppy seed cake

vanilla and coconut baked apples

banana cake

plum and chocolate clafoutis

vanilla and coconut baked apples

6 red apples
½ cup (40g/1½ oz) desiccated coconut
1 tablespoon plain (all-purpose) flour
60g (2 oz) butter, softened
3 tablespoons demerara sugar
1 vanilla bean, cut into 6 pieces

Preheat the oven to 180°C (350°F). Core apples, scooping out some of the flesh, and score around the middle of the skin. Combine coconut, flour, butter and sugar in a small bowl. Spoon the mixture into the apples and top with a piece of vanilla bean. Place the apples in a baking dish and bake for 40 minutes or until soft. Serves 6.

banana cake

125g (4 oz) butter, softened
1 cup (220g/7¾ oz) caster (superfine) sugar
¼ cup (45g/1⅔ oz) brown sugar
3 eggs
2 cups (300g/10½ oz) plain (all-purpose) flour
2 teaspoons baking powder
1 teaspoon ground cinnamon
¾ cup (190g/6¾ oz) sour cream
1 cup roughly mashed banana
caramel sauce
¾ cup (130g/4½ oz) brown sugar
1 cup (250ml/8 fl oz) (single or pouring) cream

Preheat the oven to 180°C (350°F). Place the butter, caster sugar and brown sugar in the bowl of an electric mixer and beat until light and creamy. Gradually add the eggs and beat well. Sift the flour and baking powder over the egg mixture. Add the cinnamon, sour cream and banana and stir to combine. Spoon the mixture into a lightly greased 26cm (10 in) fluted ring tin. Bake for 40 minutes or until cooked when tested with a skewer. Cool cake on a wire rack and serve with slightly cooled caramel sauce. Serves 8–10.

To make caramel sauce, combine the sugar and cream in a small saucepan over medium heat and stir until the sugar is dissolved. Increase the heat and boil for 8 minutes or until the sauce thickens.

plum and chocolate clafoutis

⅓ cup (50g/1¾ oz) plain (all-purpose) flour, sifted
¼ cup (30g/1 oz) cocoa powder, sifted
⅓ cup (75g/2⅔ oz) caster (superfine) sugar, sifted
1 teaspoon vanilla extract
3 eggs
1 cup (250ml/8 fl oz) (single or pouring) cream
1 cup roughly chopped dark chocolate
20g (¾ oz) unsalted butter, melted
8 blood plums, halved and stoned

Preheat the oven to 180°C (350°F). Place the flour, cocoa and sugar in a bowl. In a separate bowl, place the vanilla, eggs and cream and stir to combine. Add the egg mixture to the flour mixture and whisk to combine. Stir in the chocolate. Brush a 4 cup (1 litre/32 fl oz) capacity baking dish with the melted butter. Pour in the chocolate mixture, top with the plum halves and bake for 20–25 minutes or until puffed and cooked through. Serves 8.

whole orange cake and candied peel

2 oranges
175g (6 oz) butter
1½ cups (330g/11½ oz) caster (superfine) sugar
3 eggs
¾ cup (90g/3 oz) almond meal (ground almonds)
1½ cups (225g/7⅞ oz) plain (all-purpose) flour
2 teaspoons baking powder
candied peel and syrup (recipe, page 16), to serve

Preheat the oven to 160°C (320°F). Wash the oranges and place in a saucepan of water over medium heat. Bring the water to the boil, then reduce the heat and simmer the oranges for 30 minutes or until soft. Remove the oranges, cool slightly, then chop roughly. Process the oranges in a food processor until finely chopped. Add the butter, sugar, eggs, almond meal, flour and baking powder and process until smooth. Spoon the mixture into a greased and floured 24cm (9½ in) kugelhopf tin. Bake for 1 hour or until cooked when tested with a skewer. Cool in the tin for 10 minutes then remove and cool on a wire rack. Serve with candied peel and syrup. Serves 8–10.

whole orange cake and candied peel

cheesecakes with crushed raspberries

crushed raspberry sauce
200g (7 oz) fresh or frozen raspberries
1 cup sugar
base
55g (1⅞ oz) plain sweet biscuits
⅓ cup (40g/1½ oz) almond meal (ground almonds)
30g (1 oz) butter, melted
filling
600g (20 oz) cream cheese, softened
¾ cup (190g/6¾ oz) sour cream
2 eggs
1 cup (220g/7¾ oz) caster (superfine) sugar
1 teaspoon vanilla extract

Preheat the oven to 200°C (400°F). To make crushed raspberry sauce, place the raspberries in an ovenproof dish and sprinkle with sugar. Bake for 15 minutes or until mixture is syrupy. Set aside.

To make the base, process biscuits in a food processor until finely chopped. Add the almond meal and butter and process until combined. Grease 6 x ¾ cup (185ml/6 fl oz) capacity non-stick muffin tins. Line each tin with 2 intersecting strips of non-stick baking paper. Press the crumb mixture into the bases of the tins and refrigerate. Preheat the oven to 140°C (285°F).

To make filling, process cream cheese, sour cream, eggs, sugar and vanilla in a food processor until smooth. Pour mixture over bases and bake for 30 minutes. Chill, serve with raspberry sauce. Makes 6.

lime and mango coconut cake

4 eggs
1 cup (220g/7¾ oz) sugar
1 cup (150g/5¼ oz) self-raising (self-rising) flour
150g (5¼ oz) butter, melted
1 cup (75g/2⅔ oz) dessicated coconut
1 teaspoon finely grated lime rind
lime and mango topping
½ cup (110g/3¾ oz) sugar
¾ cup (185ml/6 fl oz) water
1 tablespoon lime juice
1 vanilla bean, split and seeds scraped
3 mangoes, thinly sliced

To make topping, place the sugar, water, lime juice and vanilla bean and seeds in a deep frying pan over low heat. Stir until sugar is dissolved then simmer for 3–4 minutes. Add the mango and cook for 6–7 minutes or until lime vanilla mixture is syrupy. Remove mango with a slotted spoon, reserving the syrup, and arrange on the base of a lightly greased 22cm (8½ in) cake tin.

Preheat the oven to 160°C (320°F). Place eggs and sugar in the bowl of a mixer and beat for 8 minutes or until tripled in volume. Sift the flour over the egg mixture and fold through. Fold through the butter, coconut and lime rind. Spoon mixture over mango. Bake for 45 minutes or until cooked when tested. Stand in tin for 10 minutes before turning out. Serve with warmed syrup with vanilla bean removed. Serves 8.

cheesecakes with crushed raspberries

lime and mango coconut cake

blueberry muffins

apple and cinnamon tea cake

summer nectarine cakes

blueberry muffins

2 cups (300g/10½ oz) self-raising (self-rising) flour
½ cup (110g/3¾ oz) caster (superfine) sugar
2 eggs
⅓ cup (80ml/2½ fl oz) vegetable oil
1 cup (250g/8 oz) sour cream
1 cup fresh or frozen blueberries

Preheat the oven to 180°C (350°F). Combine the flour, sugar, eggs, oil and sour cream in a medium bowl and mix well. Sprinkle the mixture with the blueberries and stir to combine. Spoon the blueberry mixture into lightly greased 1 cup (250ml/8 fl oz) capacity muffin tins. Bake for 25–30 minutes or until cooked through. Makes 6.

apple and cinnamon tea cake

185g (6½ oz) butter, softened
½ teaspoon ground cinnamon
⅔ cup (150g/5¼ oz) caster (superfine) sugar
3 eggs
1½ cups (225g/7⅞ oz) plain (all-purpose) flour
½ teaspoon baking powder
⅓ cup (80ml/2½ fl oz) milk
topping
4 small green apples, peeled, halved and cored
1 teaspoon sugar
¼ teaspoon ground cinnamon
¼ cup apricot jam (jelly), warmed

Preheat the oven to 160°C (320°F). Place the butter, cinnamon and sugar in the bowl of an electric mixer and beat until light and creamy. Gradually add the eggs and beat well. Sift the flour and baking powder over the butter mixture, add the milk and stir until combined. Line the base of a 22cm (8½ in) springform tin with non-stick baking paper and spoon in the mixture.

To make the topping, cut a row of deep slits in each apple half and arrange over the top of the cake mixture. Combine the sugar and cinnamon and sprinkle over the apples. Bake for 50 minutes. Brush the cake with the warm jam and return to the oven for 10 minutes or until cooked when tested with a skewer. Serve warm. Serves 8–10.

summer nectarine cakes

3 egg whites
1 cup (110g/3¾ oz) almond meal (ground almonds)
½ cup (75g/2⅔ oz) icing (confectioner's) sugar, sifted
¼ cup (40g/1½ oz) self-raising (self-rising) flour
50g (1¾ oz) butter, melted
1 tablespoon finely grated lemon rind
1 large nectarine, halved and thinly sliced

Preheat the oven to 180°C (350°F). Place egg whites, almond meal, sugar, flour, butter and lemon rind in a bowl and mix to combine. Spoon 1 tablespoon of the mixture into 12 lightly greased ¼ cup (60ml/2 fl oz) capacity patty tins and top with a slice of nectarine. Bake for 15 minutes or until puffed and golden. Makes 12.

apricot slice

9 egg whites
3 cups (330g/11½ oz) almond meal (ground almonds)
1½ cups (225g/7⅞ oz) icing (confectioner's) sugar
1½ cups (225g/7⅞ oz) self-raising (self-rising) flour
150g (5¼ oz) unsalted butter, melted
3 tablespoons finely grated orange rind
1kg (2¼ lb) apricots, halved and stoned
½ cup (110g/3¾ oz) white sugar

Preheat the oven to 180°C (350°F). Place the egg whites, almond meal, icing sugar, flour, butter and orange rind in a bowl and stir well to combine. Place the apricots and sugar in a bowl and toss well to coat. Spoon the egg white mixture into a lightly greased 25 x 35cm (10 x 13¾ in) baking dish and top with the apricots. Bake for 40–45 minutes or until the apricot slice is cooked when tested with a skewer. Serves 12.

apricot slice

blueberry swirl cheesecake

220g (7¾ oz) fresh or frozen blueberries+
¼ cup (55g/1⅞ oz) caster (superfine) sugar
base
85g (2⅞ oz) shortbread biscuits
½ cup (55g/1⅞ oz) almond meal (ground almonds)
45g (1⅔ oz) butter, melted
filling
600g (20 oz) cream cheese, softened
¾ cup (190g/6¾ oz) sour cream
2 eggs
1 cup (220g/7¾ oz) caster (superfine) sugar
1 teaspoon vanilla extract

Preheat the oven to 140°C (280°F). Process the blueberries in a food processor and press through a sieve (you should have ½ cup (125ml/4 fl oz) puree). Place the puree and sugar in a small saucepan over medium heat and stir until the sugar is dissolved. Increase the heat and simmer rapidly for 8 minutes or until thick. Set aside to cool.

To make the base, process the biscuits in a food processor until crushed. Add the almond meal and butter and process until combined. Grease a 22cm (8½ in) springform tin and line the base with non-stick baking paper. Press the crumb mixture over the base and refrigerate.

To make the filling, process the cream cheese in a food processor until smooth. Add the sour cream, eggs, sugar and vanilla and process until combined and smooth. Pour the cream cheese mixture over the base. Drizzle the blueberry mixture over and swirl lightly through cream cheese mixture with a butter knife. Bake for 1 hour or until set. Refrigerate and serve cold. Serves 10–12.

+ If using frozen blueberries there is no need to defrost them first.

banana and date bread

125g (4 oz) unsalted butter, softened
1 cup (175g/6 oz) brown sugar
2 eggs
1½ cups (225g/7⅞ oz) plain (all-purpose) flour, sifted
1 teaspoon baking powder, sifted
½ teaspoon bicarbonate of soda (baking soda)
¼ teaspoon ground nutmeg
¼ teaspoon ground cinnamon
1½ cups mashed banana
¼ cup (60ml/2 fl oz) maple syrup
1 cup chopped dates

Preheat the oven to 160°C (320°F). Place the butter and sugar in the bowl of an electric mixer and beat until pale and creamy. Gradually add the eggs and beat well. Fold through the flour, baking powder, bicarbonate of soda, nutmeg and cinnamon and stir well to combine. Stir in the banana, maple syrup and dates. Spoon the mixture into a lightly greased 7 x 32cm (2¾ x 12½ in) loaf tin lined with non-stick baking paper. Bake for 1 hour and 10 minutes or until cooked when tested with a skewer. Allow the banana bread to cool in the tin and slice to serve. Serves 6–8.

blueberry swirl cheesecake

banana and date bread

glossary, index

+ conversions

almond meal

Also known as ground almonds, almond meal is available from most supermarkets. Used instead of, or as well as, flour in cakes and desserts. Make your own by processing whole, skinned almonds to a fine meal in a food processor or blender (125g/4 oz almonds will give 1 cup almond meal). To remove the skins from almonds, briefly soak in boiling water, then, using fingers, slip skins off.

butter

Unless stated otherwise in a recipe, butter should be at room temperature for cooking. It should not be half-melted or too soft to handle, but should still have some "give" when pressed. When using butter to make pastry, it should be cold and chopped into small pieces so that it can be evenly distributed throughout the flour. Although most bakers use unsalted rather than salted butter, it is a matter of personal preference and does not make much difference to the outcome. Salted butter has a much longer shelf-life, which makes it preferable for some people. Store butter in the fridge away from other foods with odours, mild or strong, as it is very easily tainted.

buttermilk

Originally the liquid left over when butter was churned, buttermilk is low-fat milk cultured with lactic acid to produce a tangy liquid which is used in baking, pancakes, dressings and as a tenderiser.

brioche

A sweet French yeast bread made in loaf or bun form, traditionally dunked in coffee at breakfast. Brioche is available from speciality bread and cake stores and some supermarkets.

caramelising sugar

spoon method

Also known as brûléeing, rest the back of the bowl of a spoon on an open gas flame for 5 minutes or until very hot. Using a thick tea towel, lift the handle and run the spoon over sugar topping. Caramelisation will happen instantly and the sugar will set to hard toffee. The spoon will turn permanently black after heating.

blowtorch method

Light the blowtorch and carefully hold the flame 2cm (¾ in) above the sugar coating and heat for 1 minute or until the sugar begins to bubble and caramelise.

cream

The fat content determines the names of the different types of cream and the uses for which they are ideal.

single or pouring cream

Has a butter fat content of 20–30 per cent. It is the type of cream most commonly used for making ice-cream, panna cotta and custard. It can also be whipped to a light and airy consistency.

thickened cream

Not to be mistaken for heavy or double cream (below), this is single or pouring cream that has had a vegetable gum added to stabilise it. The gum makes the cream a little thicker and easier to whip.

heavy or double cream

Has a butter fat content of 40–50 per cent. It's often served with cakes and desserts.

eggs

The standard egg size used in this book is 59g (2 oz). It is very important to use the right size eggs for a recipe, as this will affect the outcome of baked goods. The correct volume is especially important when using egg whites to make meringues. Use eggs at room temperature for baking, so remember to take them from the fridge about 30 minutes before you begin.

gelatine

A thickening or setting agent made from collagen (a protein found in animal connective tissue and bones) and sold in both leaf and powdered forms. Powdered gelatine is available from supermarkets and should be dissolved in liquid over warm water before adding to the liquid it is to set. Leaf gelatine is available from speciality food stores. It comes in various grades or strengths including silver, titanium, platinum and gold. Because of the varying setting strengths, take care to follow the instructions on the package regarding how many leaves are required to set a given volume of liquid. Leaves should be softened in cold water for 5 minutes before squeezing out excess and adding to the mixture to be set. Agar agar is a vegetarian gelatine substitute.

jam pan

Use a deep-sided pan to reduce the risk of boiling jam splattering out. Traditional preserving pans have a wide base to allow the jam to boil faster, which speeds up evaporation and retains the fruit's flavour. Substitute with a heavy-based deep frying pan. Even heat from the pan's heavy base reduces the risk of the jam burning and sticking to the pan.

lemongrass

A tall lemon-scented grass used in Asian cooking. Peel away the outer leaves before chopping or slicing the tender root end. Available from Asian food stores, most supermarkets and greengrocers.

mascarpone cheese

A fresh Italian triple-cream curd-style cheese. Its consistency is similar to thick (double) cream and it is used in a similar way in cakes, desserts and sauces. Available from supermarkets, speciality food stores and many delicatessens.

muscat

A dessert wine sometimes referred to as "liquid sunshine" because the grapes are left to ripen well beyond normal maturity before harvesting. The resulting intense toffee-flavoured wine is enhanced by fortification with brandy and ageing in oak.

panna cotta

2 tablespoons powdered gelatine
⅓ cup (80ml/2½ fl oz) water
3¾ cups (935ml/30 fl oz) (single or
   pouring) cream
1 cup (150g/5¼ oz) icing (confectioner's)
   sugar
1 teaspoon vanilla extract

Sprinkle the gelatine over the water and set aside for 5 minutes. Place the cream, icing sugar and vanilla in a saucepan over medium heat and stir. Add the gelatine mixture and simmer over low heat for 4 minutes or until dissolved. Allow the mixture to cool to room temperature then pour into moulds and refrigerate for 6 hours or overnight. To serve, dip the moulds in warm water and invert the panna cottas onto plates.

pastry

Make your own or, if time is at a premium, use one of the many store-bought fresh or frozen varieties.

puff pastry

Time-consuming and difficult to make. Available from patisseries (order a block in advance) or use the frozen supermarket variety, in block form if possible, so you can roll it out to the thickness you need. If using store-bought sheets, you may need to layer several to the required thickness.

sweet shortcrust pastry

2 cups (300g/10½ oz) plain
   (all-purpose) flour
3 tablespoons caster (superfine) sugar
150g (5 oz) cold butter, chopped
2–3 tablespoons iced water

Process the flour, sugar and butter in a food processor until the mixture resembles rough breadcrumbs. While the motor is running, add enough iced water to form a smooth dough and process until just combined. Knead the dough lightly, wrap in plastic wrap and refrigerate for 30 minutes. Roll out the pastry on a lightly floured surface or between sheets of non-stick baking paper until 2–3mm (⅛ in) thick, or whatever thickness required, and line the tart tin. (This recipe makes about 350g (12¼ oz) pastry, which is sufficient to line up to a 26cm (10 in) pie dish or tart tin.) Preheat the oven to 180°C (350°F). Place a piece of non-stick baking paper over the pastry and fill with baking weights or uncooked rice or beans. Bake pastry for 10 minutes, remove the weights and bake for a further 10 minutes or until the pastry is golden. Spoon in the filling and bake again as the recipe indicates.

sponge cake

⅔ cup (100g/3½ oz) plain flour
¼ teaspoon baking powder
4 eggs
½ cup (110g/3¾ oz) caster
   (superfine) sugar
50g (1¾ oz) butter, melted

Preheat the oven to 180°C (350°F). Sift the flour and baking powder three times. Set aside. Place the eggs and sugar in the bowl of an electric mixer and beat for 8–10 minutes or until thick and pale and tripled in volume. Sift the flour over the egg and sugar mixture and gently fold through using a metal spoon. Fold through melted butter. Grease a 20cm (8 in) square tin and line base with non-stick baking paper. Pour the mixture into tin and bake for 25 minutes or until the cake is springy to touch and comes away from the sides of the tin. Cool on a wire rack. Serves 8–10.

sterilising jam jars

Before filling your jars with jam, it is essential to sterilise both the jars and lids. It is best to use proper preserving jars and lids available from specialty cookware stores and some department stores. Make sure the jars are free of cracks and chips. To sterilise the jam jars and lids, wash them in hot, soapy water then rinse. Place the jars and lids upside down on a baking tray lined with a clean tea towel and heat in a preheated 100°C (212°F) oven for 15 minutes or until dry. To prevent the jars from cracking, pour the hot jam into the jars while the jars are hot. Seal with lids.

still-freezing method

If you don't have an ice-cream maker, you can use the still-freezing method to freeze your ice-cream in the freezer. Pour the cooled custard into a metal bowl and place in the freezer for 2½ hours or until set around the edges but soft in the middle. Beat with an electric hand mixer and return the ice-cream to the freezer for 3–4 hours or until firm. Repeat the beating and freezing process once more.

sugar

Extracted as crystals from the juice of the sugar cane plant or beet, sugar is a sweetener, flavour enhancer, bulking agent and preservative. It makes ice-cream and custards smoother and keeps cakes moist.

brown sugar

Sugar that has been processed with molasses. It comes in differing shades of brown, according to the quantity of molasses added, which varies between countries. This also affects the taste of the sugar, and therefore the end product. The brown sugar referred to in this book is sometimes also called light brown sugar. For a richer taste you can substitute dark brown sugar.

caster (superfine) sugar

Its finer grain gives baked products a light texture and crumb, which is important for many cakes and light desserts such as meringues in which the sugar must be completely dissolved.

demerara sugar

A brown, crystallised cane sugar with a mild caramel flavour. Suitable for use in cooking. Available from speciality food stores and most supermarkets. If demerara sugar is unavailable, you can substitute with 3 parts white sugar mixed with 1 part brown sugar.

icing (confectioner's) sugar

Is regular granulated sugar ground to a very fine powder. It often clumps together and needs to be pressed through a fine sieve before using. Always use pure icing (confectioner's) sugar not an icing sugar mixture, which contains cornflour (cornstarch) and needs more liquid.

regular granulated white sugar

Is used in baking when a light texture is not crucial to the outcome. Because the crystals are quite large, you need to beat, add liquids to, or heat regular sugar to dissolve it.

sugar syrup and caramel

When making sugar syrup or caramel from sugar and water, it is important to stir the mixture so that the sugar dissolves before the mixture bubbles. Also, wipe down the inside of the saucepan with a pastry brush that has been dipped into water to remove any sugar crystals. This will help to give you a clear syrup that will not crystallise.

tins

Aluminium (aluminum) tins are fine but stainless steel will last longer and won't warp or buckle. Measure tin widths at the open top, not at the base. If the tin has a lip, measure from the inside of the lip.

bundt tins

Come in smooth and fluted versions. Whatever the shape, always grease the tin well. To remove a cake, loosen it with a palette knife and give it a slight twist.

fluted tart tins

Are available in individual-serve to large sizes, may be deep or shallow, and come with or without removable bases. The standard sizes are 10, 20 and 24cm (4, 8 and 9½ in). Opt for the removable base for easy removal of delicate crusts, especially when using a larger tart tin.

muffin tins

The standard sizes are a 12 hole tin, each hole with ½ cup (125ml/4 fl oz) capacity, or a 6 hole tin, each hole with 1 cup (250ml/8 fl oz) capacity. Great for making individual cakes and muffins. Non-stick tins make for easy removal, or line with paper patty cases.

patty tins

These come in a variety of sizes but the standard is 2 tablespoon capacity. There are also shallow patty tins which are great for small tarts and pies. Grease the tins well before using or line them with paper patty cases for easy removal.

round tins

The standard sizes for round tins are 18, 20, 22 and 24cm (7, 8, 8½ and 9½ in). The 20 and 24cm (8 and 9½ in) round tins are the must-haves of the range.

slice tins

The standard slice tin size is 20 x 30cm (8 x 12 in). These tins are great for slices or large slab cakes as well as roulades and Swiss rolls.

springform tins

The standard sizes are 20, 23 and 24cm (8, 9 and 9½ in). The best tin to use for delicate cakes such as cheesecakes, mud cakes and layer cakes. The spring-loaded side collar lifts away, allowing for removal of the cake without the need to invert.

square tins

The standard sizes for square tins are 18, 20, 22 and 24cm (7, 8, 8½ and 9½ in). If you have a recipe for a cake cooked in a round tin and you want to use a square tin, the general rule is to subtract 2cm (about 1 in) from the size of the tin. So you would need a 20cm (8 in) square tin for a recipe calling for a 22cm (8½ in) round cake tin.

tart rings

These metal rings sit flat on a lined baking tray and are used for cooking tarts with a straight side. Simply lift the ring away at the end of baking. Available from speciality cookware shops.

vanilla beans

These cured pods from the vanilla orchid are used whole, usually split with the tiny seeds scraped into the mixture, to infuse flavour into custard and cream-based recipes. If unavailable, substitute 1 vanilla bean with 1 teaspoon pure vanilla extract (a thick, sticky liquid – not to be confused with vanilla essence).

vanilla extract

For a pure vanilla taste, use a good-quality vanilla extract, not an essence or imitation flavour, or use a vanilla bean.

conversion chart

1 teaspoon = 5ml
1 Australian tablespoon = 20ml (4 teaspoons)
1 UK tablespoon = 15ml (3 teaspoons/½ fl oz)
1 cup = 250ml (8 fl oz)

liquid conversions

metric	imperial	cups
30ml	1 fl oz	⅛ cup
60ml	2 fl oz	¼ cup
80ml	2½ fl oz	⅓ cup
125ml	4 fl oz	½ cup
185ml	6 fl oz	¾ cup
250ml	8 fl oz	1 cup
375ml	12 fl oz	1½ cups
500ml	16 fl oz	2 cups
600ml	20 fl oz	2½ cups
750ml	24 fl oz	3 cups
1 litre	32 fl oz	4 cups

cup measures

1 cup almond meal	110g	3¾ oz
1 cup sugar, brown	175g	6 oz
1 cup sugar, white	220g	7¾ oz
1 cup caster (superfine) sugar	220g	7¾ oz
1 cup icing (confectioner's) sugar	150g	5¼ oz
1 cup plain (all-purpose) flour	150g	5¼ oz
1 cup cocoa powder	120g	3¾ oz

a

almond
+ mango tart 58
+ peach cakes 72
pear tart 66
apple
+ cinnamon tea cake 82
pie 64
tart 60
apples, vanilla + coconut baked 76
apricot
slice 82
turnovers 66

b

baked apples, vanilla + coconut 76
banana
blueberry pancakes 22
cake 76
+ date bread 84
fritters with maple syrup 22
teacup puddings 46
berries + figs in vanilla syrup 36
berry
breakfast 22
+ brioche bake 72
bircher muesli 26
blackcurrant + rhubarb pies 64
blistered plum + mascarpone tart 60
blood orange
marmalade 28
tart 64
blueberry
banana pancakes 22
muffins 82
swirl cheesecake 84
bread, banana + date 84
breakfast muffins 26
brioche + berry bake 72

c

cake
apple + cinnamon tea cake 82

banana 76
blueberry swirl cheesecake 84
lemon with passionfruit syrup 72
lime + mango coconut 78
orange with candied peel 76
orange + poppy seed 72
sponge 89
cakes (small)
cheesecakes with crushed raspberries 78
nectarine 82
peach + almond 72
caramelised apple tart 60
caramelising sugar 88
cheesecake, blueberry swirl 84
cheesecakes with crushed raspberries 78
chocolate + plum clafoutis 76
cinnamon
+ apple tea cake 82
pear pies 58
clafoutis, plum + chocolate 76
coconut
cake, with lime + mango 78
+ vanilla baked apples 76
crème brûlée with passionfruit topping 46
crumble, rhubarb + vanilla 46
crushed raspberry tart 54

d

date + banana bread 84

f

fig tarts with brown sugar mascarpone 64
figs + berries in vanilla syrup 36
filling
raspberry cream 36
sour cream 54
vanilla cream 48
vanilla mascarpone 60
free-form rhubarb + blackcurrant pies 64
French toast, nectarine 26
fritters, banana with maple syrup 22
fruit
galettes 40

salad with lemongrass syrup, yoghurt
+ pistachios 22
sorbet 40

g

galettes, fruit 40
granola, nectarine 26

i

ice-cream
raspberry semifreddo 40
still-freezing method 89
strawberry 42

j

jams + preserves
blood orange marmalade 28
peach + passionfruit jam 30
rhubarb + vanilla jam 30
sterilising jam jars 89
strawberry jam 28
jelly, raspberry + rosé 48

l

lemon
cake with passionfruit syrup 72
soufflé 36
tart 58
lime + mango coconut cake 78

m

mango
+ almond tart 58
+ lime coconut cake 78
sorbet — see fruit sorbet 40
marmalade, blood orange 28
mascarpone + blistered plum tart 60
meringue, pavlova 42
mixed berry breakfast 22
muesli, bircher 26
muffins
blueberry 82
breakfast 26

n

nectarine
  cakes 82
  French toast 26
  granola 26

o

orange
  cake + candied peel 76
  marmalade 28
  + poppy seed cake 72
  syrup 72
  tart 64

p

pancakes, blueberry banana 22
panna cotta 89
  peach + vanilla 40
passionfruit
  + peach jam 30
  soufflé 48
pavlova 42
peach
  + almond cakes 72
  how to peel 17
  + passionfruit jam 30
  + plum pie 54
  + vanilla panna cotta 40
pear
  + almond tart 66
  + cinnamon pies 58
  poached 46
peel
  candied 16
  zesting + grating 16
peeling stonefruit 17
pie
  apple 64
  peach + plum 54
pies (small)
  cinnamon pear 58
  rhubarb + blackcurrant 64
pineapple tarte tatin 54

plum
  + chocolate clafoutis 76
  + mascarpone tart 60
  + peach pie 54
poached
  pears 46
  summer fruits 36
preserves — see jams + preserves
puddings, banana teacup 46

q

quince tarte tatin 58

r

raspberry
  + rosé jelly 48
  semifreddo 40
  sorbet — see fruit sorbet 40
  tart 54
rhubarb
  + blackcurrant pies 64
  crumble tarts 54
  + vanilla crumble 46
  + vanilla jam 30
rosé + raspberry jelly 48
rustic peach + plum pie 54

s

sauces + syrups
  brandy syrup 60
  caramel sauce 76
  orange syrup 72
  passionfruit syrup 72
  raspberry sauce 78
semifreddo, raspberry 40
shortcrust pastry, sweet 89
simple peach + almond cakes 72
slice, apricot 82
sorbet, fruit 40
soufflé
  lemon 36
  passionfruit 48
sponge cake 89

sterilising jam jars 89
strawberry
  ice-cream 42
  jam 28
summer
  fruits, poached 36
  nectarine cakes 82
  trifle 36
sweet shortcrust pastry 89
syrups — see sauces + syrups

t

tart
  almond pear 66
  apple, caramelised 60
  blood orange 64
  lemon 58
  mango + almond 58
  pineapple tarte tatin 54
  plum + mascarpone 60
  quince tarte tatin 58
  raspberry 54
tarts (small)
  fig with brown sugar mascarpone 64
  rhubarb crumble 54
tea cake, apple + cinnamon 82
teacup banana puddings 46
trifle, summer 36
turnovers, apricot 66

v

vanilla
  + coconut baked apples 76
  + peach panna cotta 40
  + rhubarb crumble 46
  + rhubarb jam 30

w

whole orange cake + candied peel 76

A new series of clever and simple recipes
from Australia's no. 1 cookbook author.

crispy chicken salad

¼ cup (60ml/2 fl oz) oyster sauce
1 tablespoon soy sauce
2 tablespoons plain (all-purpose) flour
cracked black pepper
4 x 140g (5 oz) chicken thigh fillets, thinly sliced
1 tablespoon olive oil
1 cucumber, thinly sliced
1 cup bean sprouts
1 cup coriander (cilantro) leaves
1 cup mint leaves
2 tablespoons lime juice

Preheat a medium non-stick frying pan over medium–high heat.
Combine the oyster sauce, soy, flour and pepper. Add the chicken
and toss to coat. Add the oil and chicken to the pan and cook for
2–3 minutes each side or until crispy and cooked through. To serve,
toss the chicken with the cucumber, bean sprouts, coriander, mint
and lime juice. Serves 4.

Start your collection today.
Available from your favourite bookseller.